BOOKS BY MONA VAN DUYN

TO SEE, TO TAKE

TO SEE, TO TAKE

Poems by

MONA VAN DUYN

ATHENEUM   *New York*

1971

I wish to thank the National Foundation for the Arts for a generous grant which made possible both the time and the travel that some of these poems required.

Homework, Birthday Card for a Psychiatrist, Open Letter from a Constant Reader, The Wish to Be Believed, What I Want To Say, The Good Man, The Challenger, The Creation, Advice to a God, and *Eros to Howard Nemerov* appeared in POETRY. The last three of these poems received the Harriet Monroe Memorial Prize from POETRY and the Hart Crane and Alice Crane Williams Memorial Award from The American Weave Press.

First Flight, Leda, In the Cold Kingdom, A Day in Late October, Into Mexico, Colorado, Relationships, Leda Reconsidered, and *Along the Road* appeared in THE QUARTERLY REVIEW OF LITERATURE.

Outlandish Agon (under the title *Death of a Poet*), *Causes,* and *A Spell of Conjunctivitis* appeared in POETRY NORTHWEST.

Other poems in these pages have appeared in the CARLETON MISCELLANY, CHELSEA, THE KENYON REVIEW, THE MALAHAT REVIEW, PEBBLE #3, THE POETRY BAG, THE SOUTHERN REVIEW, TAMBOURINE, and WHETSTONE.

Causes was republished in The Borestone Mountain Awards BEST POEMS OF 1966; *The Twins* received first prize in The Borestone Mountain Awards BEST POEMS OF 1967.

In one of Shakespeare's beautiful insights into human possibility, Prospero casts off his cloak of magical, all-powerful paternity and bequeaths to Miranda a world transfigured merely by romantic love. The modern Prospero, inspired by a popularized psychology, more frequently ". . . strips down to his underpants/ to teach Miranda that fathers can be informal." Somewhere between these two versions of magic appear the transformations of poetry, small, desperate and precious. I dedicate this book to poets, to the brave, new ground they continuously try to establish.

CONTENTS

Contents

I

"Time that is intolerant . . ."

OUTLANDISH AGON

There was something obscene about wrestling that baby-faced
    boy.
Women don't usually wrestle, except for a comic or grotesque
    effect,
but this was a fight for my life—I recognized him instantly.
I keep thinking how it must have looked, with him half my
    height,
and so slippery with sweat I couldn't keep hold, even with my
    nails,
and I'd hold his head back by the curls so he couldn't reach my
    own hair.
Once when we were locked together on the floor, his face
was right under mine. I looked into his tea-colored eyes
and saw clear through them to the blank bottom of the teacup.
It startled me so much I let go and rolled away,
and then he rolled on top of me. I felt his little genitalia pressing,
cool, and hard as marble. It was only for a moment.
What was dreadful was catching glimpses of freckles and a cute
    nose,
and dimples at the base of each fat, fierce finger.

My life—it was all I could have wanted, after I left home.
I held my spotted wand before the copulating world,
and it threw forth images ring-straked, speckled and grisled.
·I believed in the power of words, both birthright and blessing.
I'd make a name for myself sooner or later,
and I could trust the men in my life to sit tight on household
    matters;
in some ways they are more domestic than women.

I was surprised at my own endurance. At one point I felt
the gristle of his nose give in under my palm and his eyelids
leak under my gouging nails. I would have killed him then,
really and truly killed him once and for all,
if I could have. But he got loose a little and somehow touched me.

3

Outlandish Agon

A long time ago I'd felt intimations of that strength,
in my mother's obsessed preference, her almost professional
     tricks,
in my father's preempted eyes, which couldn't meet my eyes.

Have you ever really fought all night? All that I'd call fight
took place in the first half hour. The rest of the time
we were only clutching and wiggling a little, and even so
I don't quite know how I managed to hang on.
Now that it's over I am blessed, if you can call it that,
and the shrivelled world squeaks in rust or pain when it moves.
His strength—I can't describe it—it was not muscular,
in fact he felt soft under the sweat, like soft rubber.
But I believe in his power, beyond the power of words,
beyond himself even, flexed in my own belief.

A CHRISTMAS CARD, AFTER THE ASSASSINATIONS

What is to be born already fidgets on the stem,
near where the old leaves loosened, resembling them,
or burns in the cell, ready to be blue-eyed,
or, in the gassy heavens, gathers toward a solid,
except for that baby mutant, Christ or beast,
who forms himself from a wish, our best or last.

CAUSES

"Questioned about why she had beaten her spastic child to death, the mother told police, 'I hit him because he kept falling off his crutches.'" NEWS ITEM

Because one's husband is different from one's self,
the pilot's last words were "Help, my God, I'm shot!"
Because the tip growth on a pine looks like Christmas tree candles,
cracks appear in the plaster of old houses.

And because the man next door likes to play golf,
a war started up in some country where it is hot,
and whenever a maid waits at the bus-stop with her bundles,
the fear of death comes over us in vacant places.

It is all foreseen in the glassy eye on the shelf,
woven in the web of notes that sprays from a trumpet,
announced by a salvo of crackles when the fire kindles,
printed on the nature of things when a skin bruises.

And there's never enough surprise at the killer in the self,
nor enough difference between the shooter and the shot,
nor enough melting down of stubs to make new candles
as the earth rolls over, inverting billions of houses.

"THE WISH TO BE BELIEVED"

It is never enough to know what you want.
The brick in your hand, dampened but solid, crumbles,
and a boundary being built, in the midst of building,
stops. (Why shouldn't one say what it is like?
How would they ever know, otherwise?)

You find in your pocket a key, two keys,
one with a curlicued stem, heavy, absurd,
the other perfectly blank, anonymous.
Who knows what they open; you glance at keyholes.
It is like—you can't, after all, say exactly.

And the rooms, supposing you enter them calmly,
are different from your own; one is bare,
with a gilt-framed mirror facing the door.
Suppose you are tempted to insert your face—
you see a face, and the door closing.

And you go on past the half-built boundary,
clicking the keys together, entering.
And you reach, finally, a plain, absolute place,
and stand in the center, saying to someone,
"Believe. Believe this is what I see."

FIRST FLIGHT

"What we do not wholly possess, is that what we love?"

I

Over forty years, and I haven't left your weather.
Pocketed like a new-born kangaroo,
I've sucked the dark particular.

This morning the road to the airport, sinking in snow,
seems nevertheless to ascend, bearing a birdbrain
whose will leads up, whose life tries to follow.

World, grandmother whose ghost stories made me run,
I think I've expressed my fondness for you before.
Under those scary sheets is a dear one.

Roommate, I hold my face over your popcorn-popper
as long as I can before I board the plane.
Your white rebuffs, never stormier,

strike eyelids closing to domestic vision.
Chiller, you roll out of my sight like a snowball
and I hop to meaningless sunshine.

II

Where am I? Quick, check the old bag
for the old baggage it feels too light to bear.
Eyes, breath, heart, are you here?

The souvenir I wanted to bring fell
seconds ago, an armload of whitened antennae,
signboards, washlines and a soap factory
just the right size, I would have held them all.

So you live *here*, then, my foreigner . . .

And now I can look. Oh Lord, why didn't you tell me,
you I guessed at, how serious, how beautiful it is,
that speechlessness below, a sleeping sea,
where, kissing its frost, endlessly, everywhere,
fallen, uttering, one angel voice, desire,
fills the air with light, the perfect blasphemy.

III
My useless education drops away.
Old paths I wore over foothills
of A&P pushcarts, a hospital door, pencils,
polish and Simplicity patterns
will clutter shut. I ran them daily
up to a classroom mesa where, greedy,
exhilarated, shivering in thin
air, I intended to learn.

Where someone said,
"I know you love me, I feel safe with you."
What did I save her from? She's dead.

Where I played for years with someone under the moon,
bouncing his joyous, pink, four-chambered ball.
But once when I caught it and lifted it to throw,
its blood in ghastly maypole
streamers ran down my arm. An eclipse.
And even as my arm turned numb, goose-pimpled white,
what could I do but hold it tight?
My foolish fingers weakened less and less,
but we barely lived through that interval of darkness.

Where into someone's pocket I slipped,
like a compact at a dance, for luck,
my little hoard, unlit,
of imagined celebration.
What lit it? Suddenly he burned.

Rocket, sparkler, pinwheel
tore at his side like fiends and
chewed his cheek.
Those screams were ours. He didn't scream,
but turned like an incandescent top.
No one could stop it,
but I would have given a life to make it stop.

Where someone liked my jokes, and I liked his.
But God of Love, what kind of joke is this?
I held his hand once, knowing it was the last time,
and that cold hand never lets go of mine.

And all the rest.
Oh, we learned, didn't we, tricky thing in the breast?

IV

The ghosts of night are joining us, shade by shade,
walking unscathed over a burning striation
until it is covered with their cool feet.

The faces around me turn toward me,
beaming, incomprehensible lamps,
saying the stranger is the best beloved.
Oddly and without consequence, I am lighted.

If the poem were to speak without its syllables,
and love's spirit step out of its skin of need,
I would tremble like this.

V

Up front, someone deals with intricacies.
I fumble for his hands.
The plane, turning from spaciousness,

will be brought down by whoever believes
earth's the right place.
Don't tell me it is I.

V I
There is no mercy in a world
that chooses this tapestry to hang.
French knots of a monomaniac
riddle the linen, red, yellow and green,
electric, without reference, without movement.
The shocked imagination tries to enter it.

It is in honor of a reunion.
Having considered dearness in its several lights,
gray scholar in a second childhood,
tipsy, tangled in a dangle of diamonds,
too dizzy to call anything by its name,
I resent this gravity.

When I touch you I know what I'm doing.
Nothing is inconsequential.
Gatsby is dead in his swimming pool.
Stupid children chart the wood with breadcrumbs.
I believe you in everything except
the smoothness of this diminishing.

I fall into your arms of towers and foliage.
At the little bump of heart on heart
you begin to tell me I couldn't have lived without you.
I look into your hard eyes
since I am home and all is forgiven,
but liar, love, I see you against the sky.

LEDA

"Did she put on his knowledge with his power
Before the indifferent beak could let her drop?"

Not even for a moment. He knew, for one thing, what he was.
When he saw the swan in her eyes he could let her drop.
In the first look of love men find their great disguise,
and collecting these rare pictures of himself was his life.

Her body became the consequence of his juice,
while her mind closed on a bird and went to sleep.
Later, with the children in school, she opened her eyes
and saw her own openness, and felt relief.

In men's stories her life ended with his loss.
She stiffened under the storm of his wings to a glassy shape,
stricken and mysterious and immortal. But the fact is,
she was not, for such an ending, abstract enough.

She tried for a while to understand what it was
that had happened, and then decided to let it drop.
She married a smaller man with a beaky nose,
and melted away in the storm of everyday life.

THE CREATION

Now that I know you are gone
I have to try, like Rauschenberg,
to rub out, line by line,
your picture, feeling as I rub
the maker's most inhuman
joy, seeing as I rub
the paper's slow, awful return
to possibility.
Five times you screamed and won
from your short body a big boy
or a tall girl to join
the rest of us here,
and now let daughter or son
wear all that's left of your face
when this drawing's undone.

It is hard, heavy work.
The pencil indented the grain
of the paper, and I scour
a long time on a cheekbone
that doesn't want to disappear,
hoping my fingers won't learn
its line from going over and over
it. I replace your chin
with dead white.
Once, in a little vain
coquettishness, you joined
your party late, hair down
to your waist, and let the men
watch you twist it around
to a blonde rope and pin
the richness of its coils
into a familiar bun.
And now I make you bald
with my abrasion.

The hours we had to drink
before you'd put the dinner on!
My eraser's wet with sweat
as it moves on a frown
of long, tipsy decision:
were we all so drunk
it didn't matter, or should you strain
the Mornay sauce?
Already we are worn,
the eraser and I, and we
are nearing your eyes. Your garden
was what you saw each morning,
and your neighbor's, making fun
of her oversolicitude:
"I swear that woman
digs her plants up every day
to see if their roots have grown."
You tucked the ticklish roots
of half-grown youngsters, back in
and pressed the tilth around them.
Your eyes were an intervention.
You saw your words begin
a moody march to the page
when you tried to write what you'd seen
in poems you brought out one by one
to show us, getting braver
slowly—yes, too slowly. When
you finally sent some off—
too slowly—a magazine
took one and printed it
too slowly; you had just gone.
If I raise my head from this work
what I see is that the sun
is shining anyway,
and will continue to shine
no matter whose pale Dutch blue
eyes are closed or open,

no matter what graphite memories
do or do not remain,
so I erase and don't
look up again.
When I answer the phone
I don't any longer expect
your jerky conversation—
one funny little comment,
then silence until I began
trying to fill it myself;
at last the intention
would appear, "Come for dinner
and help me entertain
someone I'm scared of." It was hard
to believe you were often
really sick and afraid.
You heard the tune
of our feelings, I think,
over the phone, even.
You liked a joke.
You loved Beethoven.
And this is the end of your ear.
I see your nose redden
with summer allergies,
wrinkle at your husband's pun
and then straighten and fade.
What is left of you is graven,
almost, into one kind of smile.
I don't think I can mourn
much more than I already have
for this loved irritant—prune
pucker, with ends of lips
pulled up. More than your grin
it lasts, and with it lasts
a whole characterization
I can't dispose of
unless I rub clear through and ruin

this piece of anti-art.
When our repartee would run
too fast, or someone's anecdote
run long, or someone mention
a book you hadn't read,
that smile meant you were hidden.
It meant you needed time
to think of something clever or mean,
or that you thought we'd gone too far
from the gentle and sane.
It meant you were our wise,
dear, vulnerable, human
friend, as true and false as life
would let you be, and when
I move you that much farther from
your self to generalization
there is a blur
and your smile stops. This thing is done.

Swept empty by a cyclone
inside, I lift the paper.
But before I blow it clean,
sketched now in rubber crumbs,
another face is on it—mine,
Sneak, Poet, Mon-
ster, trying to rob you with words.

Your death was your own.

THE PIETÀ, RHENISH, 14TH C., THE CLOISTERS

He stares upward at a monstrous face,
as broad as his chest, as long as he is
from the top of his head to his heart. All her
feeling and fleshiness is there.

To be on her lap is to be all shrunken
to a little composition of bone
and held away from her upper body,
which, like an upended cot smoothed neatly

and topped with a tight, girlish bolster
of breasts, rises behind him, queer
to them both, as if no one had ever rested
upon it, or rumpled it, or pressed it.

And so it stands free of suffering.
But above it, the neck, round and wrinkling
from the downward tilt of the head it's bearing,
bears the full weight of that big thing.

It is a face that, if he could see
as we are forced to see, and if he
knew, as we cannot help but know, that
his dead, dangling, featureless, granite

feet would again have to touch the ground,
would make him go mad, would make his hand,
whose hard palm is the same size
as one of his mother's tearless eyes,

hit it, since nothing in life can cure
pain of this proportion. To see her
is to understand that into the blast
of his agony she turned, full-faced,

and the face began to melt and ache,
the brows running down from their high arc
to the cheekbone, the features falling toward the chin,
leaving the huge forehead unlined, open,

until, having felt all it could feel,
her face numbed and began to congeal
into this. With horror he'd have to see
the massive girl there, vapidly

gazing, stupid, stupefied.
If he said, "Willingly I dried
out of consciousness and turned to the slight
husk you hold on your knee, but let

an innocent, smaller love of a son
hold me, let not my first stone
be the heart of this great, grotesque mother.
Oh God, look what we've done to each other,"

then from the head her slow wit,
stirring, would speak, "My darling, it was not
I who belittled you, but love
itself, whose nature you came to believe

was pure possibility, though you came through
its bloody straits. And not you,
but love itself, has made me swell
above you, gross and virginal

at once. I touch what's left on my knee
with the tips of my fingers—it is an ugly,
cold corrugation. Here on my lap,
close in my arms, I wanted to keep

both the handsome, male load of your whole
body and the insupportable,
complete weightlessness of your loss.
The holy and incestuous

met and merged in my love, and meet
in every love, and love is great.
But unmanned spirit or unfleshed man
I cannot cradle. Child, no one can."

A DAY IN LATE OCTOBER

for Randall Jarrell

I

It is time to drive in the hills
and look at leaves,
time to envision again
the fortunate fall of light,
which must have come down this week
like a snow of angels.
Angel after angel lies with his chosen
fat little earthy color.
In those thousand thousand embraces
no one can see now
who corrupts and who illuminates. . . .

II

"If Galileo had said in verse that the earth moved,
the Inquisition might have let him alone"—so Hardy
turned from the mighty fictions. "I too dislike it. There are things
important . . ." laying her hand on the granite block of a library,
a beautiful old woman said simply, "It's cool to my hand."
Five poets live in the open ward of a Midwest city
where the paper's book page editor snorts, "Review that stuff?
That stuff's been dead for fifty years," each with his goofy,
compulsive tricks to keep from thinking, "What if it's true?"
A poet in his cups at one of those Washington, D.C.
meetings said, "It's a bunch of black marks. The rest is the
    reader's
love, goodwill or foolishness." Less and less do we
know what it is. Like the Bushmen who want to be left in peace,
one of its names would seem to be *Twa*, meaning "only" or
    "merely."

III
The helpless tribe in Iowa
could neither beat nor conjure
its little savage into line.
That child would scream at beasts,
at cows who lifted gaunt faces
to feast their bulged, hallucinating eyes
on her. When the corn grew over her head,
Reform School boys broke out
and hid in the cornrows till dark.
She hid with them. Her hand sweated
with theirs on the blooded lug wrench,
but she didn't hop the freight.
The grotesque stretched lips of friends,
the parental faces striped with clay and dung
scared her to death.
Later, reading the anthropologists,
all these became familiar.
I tell you I read that stuff for dear life.

IV
All my Quixotes, gentle Dons,
reading your books for days,
I think how the mad world turns golden
under your foolish eyes,

and of how your world once held me
and holds me still.
Those windmills would have killed me.
I believe we are real.

V
Hidden in his *emploi de temps*
is the actuality of another's life.
Over and over time goes wrong,
leaves us stuck below zero in grief,

tolls its unearthly, unbearable ding-dong,
takes the tree and leaves the leaf.

Because the human calendar
can't count more than a single spring,
can't teach even the most brilliant year
to come back twice from its wintering,
when a poet dies in late October
we learn nothing from nature, nothing.

v i
. . . Later the throats of sidewalks back home
will rasp and tickle,
be cleared,
then rasp and tickle again
until the cold they're always getting
settles in every larynx, and each forgets
what it was he wanted to say.

Before that happens, I want to say no bright or seasonal thing,
only that there is too much the incorruptible poem refuses to
swallow. At the end of each line, a clench of teeth and something
falling away—tasteless memory, irreducible hunk of love, un-
believably bitter repetition, rancid failure at feeling and naming.
And the poem's revulsions become a lost world, which also contains what cannot be imagined: your death, my death.

ADVICE TO A GOD

Before you leave her, the woman who thought you lavish,
whose body you led to parade without a blush
the touching vulgarity of the *nouveau-riche*,

whose every register your sexual coin
crammed full, whose ignorant bush mistook for sunshine
the cold, brazen battering of your rain,

rising, so little spent, strange millionaire
who feels in his loins' pocket clouds of power
gathering again for shower upon golden shower,

say to her, since she loves you, "Those as unworldly
as you are fated, and I can afford, to be
may find in Love's bed the perfect economy,

but, in all of his other places, a populace
living in fear of his management, his excess
of stingy might and extravagant helplessness.

Turn from him, Danae. I am greater by far,
whose flower reseeds without love for another flower,
whose seas part without loneliness, whose air

brightens or darkens heartlessly. By chance
I have come to you, and a progeny of events,
all that the mind of man calls consequence,

will follow my coming, slaughter and marriage, intrigue,
enchantment, definition of beauty, hag
and hero, a teeming, throwaway catalogue

of the tiniest, riskiest portion of my investment.
Yet pity your great landlord, for if I lent
so much as an ear to you, one loving tenant,

your bankrupt scream as I leave might tempt me to see
all creation in the ungainly, ungodly
throes of your individuality."

II

"Heut' oder morgen kommt der Tag,
And how shall we bear it?
Lightly, lightly."

HOMEWORK

for Jim

Lest the fair cheeks begin their shrivelling
before a keeping eye has lit on their fairness,
I pluck from the stony world some that can't cling
to stone, for a homely, transparent form to bless.

Smothering Elbertas, if not Albertines,
in the thick, scalding sweetness of my care,
I add a touch of tart malice, some spicy scenes
and stirring, and screw the lid on love's breathless jar.

There in a frieze they stand, and there they can stay
until, in the fickle world's or the jaded heart's
hunger for freshness, they are consumed away.
Oh I know, I know that, great or humble, the arts

in their helplessness can save but a few selves
by such disguises from Time's hideous bite,
and yet, a sweating Proust of the pantry shelves,
I cupboard these pickled peaches in Time's despite.

EROS TO HOWARD NEMEROV

It's funny, Howard, I never thought I'd be
exposed at a poetry reading. All this time
my best disguises have been run up in rhyme.
My capriciousness and downright perversity

are what poets usually give as the reasons why
I appear as a babe. You took another look,
and, bare though I've always been, it came as a shock
to be seen with so clear and literal an eye.

You told those kids you thought my compelling power
comes from the fact that I stand for the unborn child
who wants to be born, and my slyness, my rage, my wild
scheming and cruelty serve that blind desire.

The youngsters will soon forget it, I'll see to that,
in the gorgeous fury and mindlessness of love,
but with you, a father and a maker of poems that have
more balance, more reticence than some, I thought

I'd have this little chat to let you know
I'm as busy as ever this fruitful year of the mini
and the marijuana. I've never been able to afford any
scruples, but I'd like to tell you you're right, my bow

still shoots for the sweetest dream the human creature
can have, the dream of possibility.
My Hippie babies, conceived in LSD,
crawl through the woods and streets, and human nature,

in their dirty faces and their beautiful bare behinds,
is carried along as ever. Every nation
is afraid of explosions of atoms or population,
but I count on you to say I've enough on my hands

without taking the larger view; that other gods
who watch other things and who often get in my way
(though if I were a mortal I'd invoke them night and day—
Demeter, for instance, could do much more with *her* seeds)

must get off their butts and help at the labs and polls.
I'll keep life coming—they'll have to keep it alive—
and to do my stuff I'll use what I can of the jive
and jazz and Beatles and bennies and Twiggy girls.

But first I owe you, I guess, one glimpse at the state
of my affairs as I see them. Let's take San Francisco:
Out on the campuses things are going so-so—
nude-in or love-in, it's what is going to come out

that I'm most concerned with, naturally, and signs
are no substitute for siblings. But homefolks do well,
considering that getting home is all uphill,
and downtown I'm not discouraged by waiting lines

of tourists who come to see the transvestite bars,
then go back and blunt my arrows on The Pill.
There are people on Broadway who are my people still,
I'm still in business, I have my entrepreneurs,

and still well-filled is a bar I specially prize,
where, setting down drink after drink like a daughter of Lot,
their star attraction, The Topless Mother of Eight,
dangles her golden dugs before men's eyes.

A QUIET AFTERNOON AT HOME

Not exactly disembodied, but speaking from no mouth,
oracular, or at least cryptic—even the dog
snaps to baffled attention, his head on one side—in eloquent in-
    flections, with quite a range of feelings,
low-pitched, but rising sometimes to an almost feminine whine,
the voice of the stomach, or thereabouts, sounds in the room,
saying perhaps, Go and ask yourself whether
there is not too much roughage in the world these days.
All these upheavals and revolutions are not without cause, you
    know.
No one is perfect, granted. But you may have forgotten
that it is entirely possible to have guts and be sensitive
at the same time. Or, in more plaintive tones,
My dear ones, I've seldom been so upset. I really can't hold my
    peace
a moment longer. Call it a virus abroad in the land,
call it a poisonous, toxic miasma creeping
around the globe if you like. That will help nothing.
O, go back to the simple things. Remember the milk of human
    kindness.
Or, It is good to be reminded that not everything can be put into
    words.
The deepest syllables sound in our juices and wellsprings.
Or, there is a strong tendency in people connected with the arts
to be taken in by appearances, to swallow anything.
Are they all that innocent? Might I suggest, rather, gluttonous?
Or perhaps not saying any of these things at all.
Perhaps only speaking up for a more visceral poetry.

BILLINGS AND COOINGS FROM "THE BERKELEY BARB" (*Want-Ad Section*)

. . . Couples sought (enclose photographs please)
by couple who've expeditiously run through
(and are eager for permutations *a quatre, a seize*)
all known modes of the sweet conjunction for two.

Gay guy needs, for a few conventional
dances and such, fem Lez to pose as date,
in return for which she can really have a ball
with her butch friend at parties he'll give in private.

*How bright the scholars who use a previous schooling
to get the further enlightenment they want!*
Well-rounded girl will do it hung from the ceiling
by ropes in exchange for a used copy of Kant.

A youth who pines in his present incarnation
but remembers with pleasure being a parakeet
seeks a girl just as reluctantly human
and formerly budgerigar, for a mate.

At Blank's bar, woman who'd like the *frisson*
of sex with an ex-guru should ask for Gus.
An A.C.-D.C. will share pad with someone
similarly ambidextrous.

Boy seeks cute girlfriend to share his sack
How startling now the classic or pastoral!
and lists his qualifications to attract:
"tall, dark, sensitive, handsome, sterile."

Student who can't remember the phone number
or the face of student he met at Jack's last fall,
but can't forget the hard nipples, would like her
to dial xx (transvestites need not call).

Delights they probably never knew they could have
nineteen-year-old will guarantee to disclose
to women between fifty and sixty-five
with unusually big feet or long toes.

How dazzling love's infinite variety!
How fertile is nature in her forms of joy!
Male seeks, in the area around Berkeley,
another male whose fetish is corduroy . . .

BIRTHDAY CARD FOR A PSYCHIATRIST

Your friends come fondly to your living room
believing, my dear, that the occasion's mild.
Who still feels forty as a moral *crise*
in this, the Century of the Common Child?

Uncommon gifts, brought to mid-life in pain,
are not a prize. The age demands a cure
for tragedy and gives us brand-new charts
for taking down our psychic temperature.

Othello, of course, regrets having been aggressive,
Hamlet feels pretty silly to think he trusted
terms such as "art" and "honor" instead of "projection,"
and out on the moor King Lear feels maladjusted.

An arrogant richness of the human stuff
is not a value. Nobody wants to be
left holding the bag of himself when all the others
are a democratic homogeneity.

Prospero strips down to his underpants
to teach Miranda that fathers can be informal,
while Cleopatra, Juliet, Rosalind, Kate
fight for the golden apple labelled NORMAL.

In such a state, what laurels can poems bring,
what consolation, what wishes, what advice?
May your conflicts thin out with your hair? BE HAPPY?
We hope you're feeling well? We think you're nice?

Till Burnam Wood shall come to Dunsinane,
till time shall tell us what we really are,
till Responsibility, not Health, defines
the terms of living on this serious star,

to receive the trauma of birth and pass it on
is all we're here for. Yet we hope you realize
we're glad that forty years ago you came
to join in our neurotic enterprise.

FOOTNOTES TO THE AUTOBIOGRAPHY OF BERTRAND RUSSELL

for Viktor

I

"(we did not go to bed the first time we were lovers, as there was too much to say.)"

Once out of Eden, love learned its deviousness
and found in Word its wiliest metaphor;
so if a heart, untouched and in rich disguise,
using the lips to speak of weather and war,

should receive from another masquerading heart
conversing of war and weather, the news of its need,
both may be tempted by art for the sake of art.
A long-winded discourse no other member can read,

page after page on weather and war, may ensue,
they think, with margins of blank sophistication.
And should the pedantic body scrawl there, "How true!"
dumfounded lovers can continue the conversation.

I I

*"Her objections to [marrying] him are the following: (a) He sleeps with
7 dogs on his bed. She couldn't sleep a wink in such circumstances.
(b) . . ."*

This seems, in a world where love must take its chances,
undue distaste for the first of its circumstances.

What in so snug a sleeper could be more rare
than to sense in so snuggling a crowd something lacking there?

And it seems that the lady lacks sensitivity
to how brilliant her hymeneal reception might be:

First, on the heated bed he'd push aside
seven drowsing dogs to insert one blushing bride,

and surely all other nuptial welcome pales
before a sweet thrashing given her by seven tails!

Fourteen ears attuned to their master's voice
would attend the orisons of their master's choice

in bitches, and should some Donne-reading flea propose
a speedy union, he'd suffer twenty-eight paws.

Garlanded, guarded, graced with panting devotion,
the human pair would partake of wedded emotion,

she with unwinking eyes on the dogs, and he
jostling dogs with his old impunity

until, under his lips, her eyelids would close
and the dear beast of the heart come to discompose

the bed whereon seven pairs of canine eyes
would gaze at each other with a wild surmise.

IN THE COLD KINGDOM

"The younger brother roasted a breast of Pishiboro's elephant wife and handed Pishiboro some, which he presently ate. Then the younger brother said in a voice full of scorn. 'Oh you fool. You lazy man. You were married to meat and you thought it was a wife.'" FROM A MYTH OF THE BUSHMEN

Poised upside down on its duncecap,
a shrunken purple head,
True Blueberry,
enters its tightening frame of orange lip,
and the cream of a child's cheek is daubed with
Zanzibar Cocoa, while
   Here at the Martha Washington
   Ice Cream Store
   we outdo the Symbolistes.
a fine green trickle—
Pistachio? Mint Julep?
   Words have colors,
   and colors are tasty.
sweetens his chin.
In front of me Licorice teeters like a lump of coal
on its pinkish base of Pumpkin.
   A Rauschenberg tongue
   fondles this rich donnée,
   then begins to erase it.

Turning from all that is present
in the flesh, so to speak,
let the eye wander off to a menu,
where it can start to ingest
"Quite Sour Lemon sherbet,
topped with a stem cherry and chocolate sprinkles
   Swilling in language,

all floating in bubbly cherry phosphate
  the bloated imagination
  is urged to open still wider
  and shovel it in,
and served with a twist of pretzel."
In this world "Creamy Vanilla and
Smooth Swiss Chocolate ice creams"
can be "blended with chopped pineapple,
dark fudge sauce, ripe bananas, whipped topping,
cookies, roasted nutmeats and nippy chopped cherries."
  the Unconscious, that old hog,
  being in charge here of the
  creative act.

At about the moment my tastebuds
receive a last tickle of Gingersnap
and begin to respond to
Orange Fudge, I look at you
who have bought my ice cream cones for twenty years,
  Moving another new ice to the mouth
  we needn't remember
and look away
  it is always the same mouth
  that melts it.
My mind assembles a ribald tower
of sherbet dips, all on one cone,
Apricot, Apple, Tangerine, Peach, Prune, Lime,
and then it topples.
You are steadier than I.
You order one dip always,
or, in a dish, two dips of the same flavor.

In this hysterical brilliance of neon
   Come on, consumers,
   we've got to keep scooping
it is twelve or fifteen of us
to thirty ice creams.
   so that the creams shall not rise
   like cold lava out of their bins,
   numbing our feet, our knees,
   freezing our chests, our chins, our eyes,
Open the door, quick,
and let in two handholding adolescents.
Coping with all those glands
makes them good and hungry.
   so that, flying out of their cannisters,
   the chopped nuts
   shall not top off our Technicolor grave
   with their oily ashes.

Listen! All around us toothsome cones
are suffering demolition
down to the last, nipple-like tip.
How do we know where to stop?
Perhaps the glasses and dishes
are moulded of candy, and the counters and windows . . .
   Over your half-eaten serving of Italian Delight,
   why are you looking at me
   the way you are looking at me?

POSTCARDS FROM CAPE SPLIT

I

"What is that flower?" we asked right away. What a sight!
From the rocks of the beach all the way up the hill to our house,
and all around the house and on either side of the road,
a solid ocean of flowers, shifting in the wind, shifting
in shades of pink like strokes of a brush. Heliotrope.
Pinky-white masses of bloom on five-foot red stems.
"My father brought it here," our landlady says.
" 'Be careful of heliotrope,' they told him, 'it spreads like a
    weed.' "
It has taken the hill and the house, it is on its way down the road.
Little paths are scythed through heliotrope to the sea,
from the house to the outhouse, from the road to the house,
and a square of back yard is cut away from the flowers.
"The heliotrope is taking my raspberry patch,"
the neighbor tells us, and, snuggled in heliotrope,
the kitchen gardens fight for their viney lives,
one here, one there. You can't even see them until
you're right on their edge, leaning over the heliotrope.

II

Everything looks like the sea but the sea.
The sea looks like a lake
except when fucus is dumped on its low-tide border
like heaps of khaki laundry left out to rot—
this seems a capacity for waste that is worthy of an ocean.
But the diningroom floor looks like the sea,
wide old boards, painted dark green,
that heave and ripple in waves.
Light hits the crest of each board and gives it a whitecap.

The house saves everything,
crutches and children's sleds, painted cups without handles,

chairs without seats, dried sweetgrass, fir tips in pillows.
It must be almost as old as it looks—
the father of our seventy-year-old landlady built it.
It is buffed by the salt winds to elephant color.

One goes on vacation to housekeep another way.
I have made a chart of the tides,
which are now a part of my order for a few weeks.
I have learned the perverse ways of this house—
sink and refrigerator in the kitchen,
stove, dishes and table in the diningroom.
I have tied back white net curtains,
still creased from display in the dimestore.
I have found paths through heliotrope
to each new neighbor.

I I I
We move in a maze of villages—
Addison, East Addison, South Addison,
Machias, East Machias and Machiasport.
(The *ch* is pronounced *ch*, and not *k*.)
The lobsters and cheese are at South Addison,
the doctor, the bakery and the liquor store are at Machias,
the nearest post office and, they say, frozen chicken livers
are at Addison, the seafood cannery is at East Machias.
East Addison and Machiasport we have so far been able to ignore.

The kitchen in this house is papered in villages.
Five villages from floor to ceiling, I don't know how many
across the wall. There is no place to locate one's self.
Still, because the dog snores by the oilstove, the brown
sparrow-size birds squeak cheerily in a spruce by the outhouse,
little toy boats are out on the sea after lobsters, the sun
is warm and the heliotrope is blowing like waves,
because, my God, it *is* pleasant here,
we can surely live uncentered for three weeks,
gleaning a little from one village, a little from another.

IV

Who would believe that we could learn to cook, drink, bathe,
shave, fill the dog's bowl, the icecube tray, the vase
for wildflowers, and keep ourselves in clean clothes and towels
on two buckets of water a day? Of course we steam mussels
and lobsters in, drive the dog into, wade in, and gaze upon
the sea, and that saves on our freshwater needs.
Each morning we take our two buckets, go down the road
to the landlord's house, walk in the back door
(as we were told to do) and get our water
and a hot donut, or a story about the old times here.
But we want to be self-sufficient the rest of the day,
neither past nor people between us and the ocean,
and so we have learned this new skill for the summer.

But what a small thirst one has, in summer, for the everyday
    water,
whereas, for the salty stranger, from here to the horizon
at high tide is no more than we can drink in
in a single day.

V

There are thirty-five stalks of corn in our garden.
Our landlord is trying to raise some corn this year.
He has staked and tied every stalk
to hold it against the sea winds.
Our landlady dopes the tassels with liniment
to keep the raccoons off.
Except for its corn and its heliotrope wall,
our garden is just like others all over the Cape:
four rows of potatoes,
two rows of string beans,
one row each of peas and beets,
one row of squash,
and one row of dahlias.

The man from across the bar
brought us a sea-moss pudding
in a silver dish.

V I
Our landlord's youngest son, the lobsterman,
comes in his lobstering boots, turned halfway down,
to fix our oilstove. I am dazzled by the man in boots.
It is as if a heron stood in my diningroom.

His father sits in a rocker by his kitchen stove,
knitting the twine innards for lobster traps
and saying, "When we were young I'd go out in a skiff,
why, right off here, and spear a half bushel of flounder
while She cooked breakfast. We had dried fish all winter,
and they was *some good*, I tell you." The day's light changes.

We drove inland a ways, through the Blueberry Barrens.
Mile after mile, from road to the far mountains
of furzy wasteland, flat. You almost miss it.
Suddenly, under that empty space, you notice
the curious color of the ground. Blue mile, blue mile,
and then a little bent-over group of Indians
creeping down string-marked aisles. Blue mile, blue mile,
and then more Indians, pushing their forked dustpans.
It looks like a race at some country picnic, but lost
in that monstrous space, under that vacant sky.

Why am I dazzled? It is only another harvest.
The world blooms and we all bend and bring
from ground and sea and mind its handsome harvests.

A SPELL OF CONJUNCTIVITIS

The act of seeing a tree is the act of pressing
an etched eyeball against the damp paper sky,
carefully, carefully, and there it hangs, a fresh print.
An elegant frame of fur defines the start as mid-trunk
and the highest achievement as a slight tapering.
But how insistently it gathers itself together,
forcing the multitudinous scratchings out of which it is composed
into a perpendicular, a tree, recognizably sycamore.
One supposes that the three great cloudy balls
hanging from its branches like fruit are not its own,
but appeared from some imperfection of the press—
though they match the frame and seem an arty improvement.

The dog leaps through hoops of fur, disappearing for a second
into a cloud that clearly contains the fourth dimension.
He reappears with a somewhat damaged solidity,
with several legs that require an instant to rejoin their body,
and three permanent patches of light on his black hide
which may be the other side of the room shining through.

The faces of my friends are on balloons that drift and rise.
When they go through my ceiling I can only imagine how high
    they are going,
one hovering, one all pure wasteless lift,
one snagging and coming free, snagging and coming free, all the
    way up,
one swelling, perhaps, in the light air.
They bounce around me, beautiful and unfathomed,
a pirate with a gray patch on his eye,
faces with missing mouths, as if this tenderness, that kooky wit
were inexpressible. I want to touch them.
How precariously they are delivered to my senses, and with what
    loss of self-containment!

IN THE HOSPITAL FOR TESTS

My mother's friend cooked for the drunk-and-disorderlies,
and so, when I was ten, I peeked at a cell,
and that's what I'd swear this room came out of—the county jail.
But here in a sweat lies a strange collection of qualities,
with me inside it, or maybe only somewhere near it,
while all the nonsense of life turns serious again—
bowel movements, chickenpox, the date of one's first menstrua-
    tion,
the number of pillows one sleeps on, postnasal drip—
"It has very high arches," I hear the resident note.
He has worked his way down over its ridges and jerks,
its strings and moistures, coursings, lumps and networks,
to the crinkled and slightly ticklish soles of its feet.
"Don't worry, if there's anything going on here," the interne
    says,
"we'll find it. I myself have lots of ideas."

Across the room, over a jungle of plants,
blooming, drooping, withering, withered and dead,
a real face watches, freckled and flat blue eyed.
Sometimes her husband visits, a man of plaid shirts
and apologetic smiles, and sometimes three red-head
little girls in stairsteps, too scared to talk out loud.

In twenty-four hours, the hefty nurse, all smiles,
carries out my urine on her hip like a jug of cider,
a happy harvest scene. My room-mate, later,
gets on a stretcher, clutching her stomach, and it wheels
her off down the halls for a catheter in her heart.
There's one chance in five hundred she'll die in the test. She'd like
to live for two more years for the children's sake.
Her husband waits in the room. He sweats. We both sweat.

She was only fifteen when they married, he says, but she told him
she was past eighteen and he didn't find out for years.
She's wheeled back, after a feverish two hours,
with black crochet on her arm. She was conscious all the time,
and could feel whatever it was, the little box, go
through her veins to the left of the chest from the right elbow.

The leukemia across the hall, the throat cancer a few doors down,
the leaky valve who has to sleep on eight pillows—
these sit on our beds and talk of the soggy noodles
they gave us for lunch, and the heat, and how long, how soon.
The room stinks of my urine and our greed.
To live, to live at all costs, that's what we want.
We never knew it before, but now we hunt
down the healthy nurses with our eyes. We gobble our food.
Intruders come from outside during visiting hours
and chatter about silly things, no longer our affairs.

"A little more blood, I'm on the trail." He'll go far,
my interne. My room-mate gets on the stretcher again;
she comes back almost dead, but they give her oxygen.
She whistles for breath, her face is swollen and sore
and dark. She spits up white rubber. The bronchoscope,
that's what it was this time, and more tests to come.
She wishes her husband had been here after this one.
They were going to do the other lung too, but they had to stop.

In the middle of the night her bed blazes white in the darkness.
Three red-headed daughters dangle from her lightcord.
The nurse holds a cup to her lips. It is absurd,
she is swallowing my poems. The air knots like a fist,
or a heart, the room presses in like a lung. It is empty
of every detail but her life. It is bright and deathly.

"You can go home this afternoon. You're all checked out."
My doctor is grinning over the obscene news.
My room-mate sits up and listens. "God only knows
what causes these things, but you've nothing to worry about."
In shame I pack my bag and make my call.
She reads a magazine while I wait for my husband.
She doesn't speak, she is no longer my friend.
We say goodbye to each other. I hope she does well.
In shame I walk past the staring eyes and their reproaches
all down the hall. I walk out on my high arches.

THE GOOD RESOLUTION

My right hand has suffered an amputation
of its fifth finger, the one with the hot nail,
the one that kept pointing across the room.
While the other four fingers sealed my lips and the thumb
asked for a hitchhike to my shoulder, it would point Away.
Now I am self-absorbed and lonesome.

Drifting in great woolly scarves in my head,
like the scene of an English thriller, a fog settles.
My head turns slowly, the fog shifts, and inside
its brow, crouched, the sweating maniac is revealed.
He froths and tightens, he starves for the white victim.
Now I am restless and in need of food.

The day extends itself, like a dog's tongue
in dreadful heat, or, like a bay bridge,
crosses ten empty islands and still keeps going.
Light dangles from the sky like a wet string.
I try to jerk it down, but it holds fast
and will not drop into interminable evening.

Who would have thought I'd be asking that old chestnut
at my age, seriously, Who Am I, demoralized
giant-killer or really furious giant?
One imagines paper dolls from a folded sheet
flipped open to a whole procession of selves, hands joined,
by this time. I can't wait and I won't cheat,

and so my simple twins lay hands on each other
and bend each other down to a compromise:
Five times daily let the screws be loosed, the failure
celebrated, and perhaps in the homely future,
tripping with a pursed mouth toward some Damascus,
I'll fall to my knees and rise up a non-smoker.

I am poured into five daily boxes, and all
my contents are fingered and re-arranged, arranged
and fingered. The screen I blow is too thin to conceal.
A mouse in the mind, trapped by its tail
in front of a mirror, keeps squeaking over and over
it never wanted to know itself *this* well!

INTO MEXICO

Past the angular maguey fields, a ride on the optic nerve,
we come to the first rest stop, and the visit begins.
It is what I have always wanted; to follow the first signs
in another language makes me weak with joy. I am brave
out back in a courtyard, by a shack that might be the toilet,
when bulging senoras bump me on the back and shoulder me.
If they look at me I do not know what they see,
since even metaphors are changed. Overhead in the heat
the skinned, outrageous body of some animal hangs from a line.
Is it rotting, or drying? I've never smelled its rawness before.
Yes, there is a stool in the shack, and soiled toilet paper
in a waist-high pile beside it. Water is in a can.

I touch the paper on the roll, it is rough, it is like . . . nothing
    else.
I am behind the eyes at last. It is as if one could by-pass
love, when the other eyes parry with a picture of one's own face,
and never arrive at marriage, either true or false,
when eyes glaze and minds are more private than ever,
but could stop in between at a point where no one
can stop. To be in one's first foreign country, in approximation,
is to be in you—or to feel what it must be like to be there.

Now it is one long agony of taking-in. From the bus
I can see inside the palings, or tin, or straw of a shelter,
and all pots, braziers and pallets are unfamiliar.
At the first market, walking in through the restless
yellow of bananas, I will go to such furnishings and handle them.
Country dogs here are yellow also, with a long body.
And all the time I have lived as if you were like me.
Now, here, I am released from that stratagem.

In the city I would never have expected a glassy hotel
to rise between little sheds of pink and orange cement,
nor men to pull down their pants and squat in the vacant
lot downtown. Sweet rolls—I am trying to taste them all,
but it will take weeks—are named for creatures and the parts
of creatures, Snails, Cheeks, Noses, Ears, Dogs.
What is that snarled bouquet of herbs a little boy drags
toward home, making a green sweep of the streets?
A woman kneels on the pavement all day to sell
six pyramids of seven cracked walnuts each.
I tongue a clay cup that tastes of dark and starch,
and buy eggs singly, since the price of one is marked on its shell.
Each noise, each name, is enchanted and necessary.
I drift in bed, astonished by faintness and nausea and chills.
I would never have felt this way—is this the way it feels?
Thousands of black beans shine near sweet potato candy.

One starves for this journey, I think, a simple sensing of what is
not thou, not it, but you—a visit behind the eyes
where the map bulges into belief, relief, presents sea,
mountains, macadam, presents a strange and willful country.

REMEDIES, MALADIES, REASONS

Her voice, that scooped me out of the games of the others
to dump me in bed at seven for twelve years,

and yelled me up to my feet if I sat on the ground,
liable to catch pneumonia, and each year penned

the feet, that wanted to walk bare, or hike
or wade, in the cramping, pygmy shoes of the chronic

invalid, intoned each time I raged or cried
the old story of how I'd nearly died

at six weeks from nursing a serum she'd taken,
so I'd never be well. Each day all over again

she saved me, pitted against rain, shine, cold, heat,
hunting in my mouth each morning for a sore throat,

laying a fever-seeking hand on my forehead
after school, incanting "Did your bowels move good?

Wrap up before you go out and don't play hard.
Are you *sure* you're not coming down with a cold? You look
    tired,"

keeping me numb on the couch for so many weeks,
if somehow a wily cough, flu or pox

got through her guard, my legs would shake and tingle,
trying to find the blessed way back to school.

Girl Scouts, green apples, tree climbs, fairs—the same
no. "But the other kids . . ." "Well, you're not like *them*."

Food was what, till I gagged, she kept poking in,
and then, with high enemas, snaked out again;

her one goose, refusing to fatten, I showed
her failure and shamed her with every bone I had.

If I screamed that I'd run away if I couldn't go,
she'd say, "All right, but that'll be the end of you,

you'll get sick and who'll pay the doctor bill?
You'll *die*, you know as well as I do you will."

I was scared to die. I had to carry a hankyful
of big white mineral pills, a new cure-all,

for months, and gulp them in classes every half hour.
They spilled on the floor in front of my favorite teacher.

A spastic went jerking by. "That's how *you'll* get
from twitching your finger all the time. Now quit it!"

A bandaged head moaned in the hospital. "Mastoid.
That's how *you'll* be if you don't stop blowing hard."

Only once, dumfounded, did she ever notice a thing
that might be thought of as strength in me. Breaking

another free yardstick from the drygoods store
on a butt and legs still bad, she found her junior

in high school fighting back till we rolled on the floor.
That night she said I wouldn't get spanked any more.

She took me to college and alerted the school nurse.
I went in without looking back. For four years

I tested each step, afraid to believe it was me
bearing like a strange bubble the health of my body

as I walked the fantastic land of the ordinary
and learned how to tear up the letters, "You *know* how I worry,

for my sake please don't do it . . . don't try it . . . don't go . . .
You *surely* wouldn't want to make me worry like I do!"

Marriage, work, books, years later, called
to help them when she and Dad both lay in bed,

I first stepped back in their house for a stay of more
than a few days. Soon she was crying "Come back here!

Don't you dare go outside that door without your sweater!"
"But it's hot out," said the innocent, visiting neighbor.

"Oh, but she's never been well, I have to keep watching
her like a hawk or she comes right down with something."

There, on my big shoulders, against such proof—
a quarter of a century of the charmed life

I'd been living outside the door—she could still see
the weak, rolling head of a death-threatened baby.

In a hundred visits and fifteen hundred letters
she's been showing herself to me for thirty years

(as well as six thousand days of retrospect)
in clear colors. I know what to expect

before I open my ears or the envelope.
She had to get up three times a night to "dope"

a sore, she "gargled and sprayed" for a week so as not
to get "what was going around." There was blood in the snot

she blew out last month. She "hawks up big gobs
of stuff" that is almost orange. All of her tubes

are blocked. Her face turned purple. Lettuce she ate
was "passed" whole, "green as grass" in the toilet.

She "came within an inch" of a "stoppage," but mineral oil
saved her from all but "a running-off of the bowel."

Sniffing her mucus or sweat or urine, she marvels
anew at how "rotten" or "rank" or "sour" it smells.

There's never been any other interesting news.
Homer of her own heroic course, she rows

through the long disease of living, and celebrates
the "blood-red" throat, the yellow pus that "squirts"

from a swelling, the taste, always "bitter as gall,"
that's "belched up," the bumps that get "sore as a boil,"

the gas that makes her "blow up tight as a drum,"
the "racing heart," the "new kind of bug," the "same

old sinus," the "god-awful cold"—all things that make
her "sick as a dog" or "just a nervous wreck."

Keeping her painstaking charts, first mariner
of such frightful seas, she logs each degree and number

("Three hundred thousand units of penicillin
he gave me last Thursday!" "I puked four times, and the last one

was *pure bile!*" "Fever way up to ninety-
nine-point-nine!") Daily, but not humbly,

she consults the eight shelves of the six-foot, steel,
crammed-with-medication oracle.

I know what she is, I know what she always was:
a hideous machine that pumps and wheezes,

suppurating, rotting, stinking, swelling,
its valves and pipes shrieking, its fluids oozing

in the open, in violent color, for students to learn
the horror, the nausea, of being human.

And yet, against all the years of vivid, never-
varying evidence, when I look at her

I see an attractive woman. And looking back,
testing the truth of a child's long-ago look,

I still see the mother I wanted, that I called to come,
coming. From the dark she rushes to my bedroom,

switching the lamp on, armed with pills, oils, drops,
gargles, liniments, flannels, salves, syrups,

waterbag, icebag. Bending over me,
giant, ferocious, she drives my Enemy,

in steamy, hot-packed, camphorated nights,
from every sickening place where he hides and waits.

Do you think I don't know how love hallucinates?

III

"*Love took my hand, and smiling did reply,*
  'Who made the eyes but I?'"

OPEN LETTER FROM A CONSTANT READER

To all who carve their love on a picnic table
or scratch it on smoked glass panes of a public toilet,
I send my thanks for each plain and perfect fable
of how the three pains of the body, surfeit,

hunger, and chill (or loneliness), create
a furniture and art of their own easing.
And I bless two public sites and, like Yeats,
two private sites where the body receives its blessing.

Nothing is banal or lowly that tells us how well
the world, whose highways proffer table and toilet
as signs and occasions of comfort for belly and bowel,
can comfort the heart too, somewhere in secret.

Where so much constant news of good has been put,
both fleeting and lasting lines compel belief.
Not by talent or riches or beauty, but
by the world's grace, people have found relief

from the worst pain of the body, loneliness,
and say so with a simple heart as they sit
being relieved of one of the others. I bless
all knowledge of love, all ways of publishing it.

THE MISER

I was out last night,
the very picture of a sneak, dark and hunched-over,
breaking and entering again.
Why do I do it?

And why, when I can afford serious residences,
do I keep to this one room?
Perhaps if I had not lost track of the difference
between the real and the ideal
it would never have happened.
I hide here almost entirely now.

When I go out, when I creep into those silent houses,
I steal newspapers.
An armload, no more than I can carry comfortably.
Sometimes they are already tied up
on the side porch or by the kitchen stove.
Nobody misses them.
They think each other or the maid
has carried them out to the street.

They say there is something intractable out there,
the Law, the Right to Privacy,
the World.
In the days when my obsession was only a wound-up toy,
squeaking and jabbering in my chest,
I could have believed them.

I sit by the window today
(There is very little space left now,
though I have left corridors wide enough to walk through
so I won't lose touch)
holding my latest on my lap,
handling them, fondling them, taking in every column.
They are becoming more and more precious.

My delusion grows and spreads.
Lately it seems to me
as I read of murders, wars, bankruptcies, jackpot winnings,
the news is written in that perfect style
of someone speaking to the one
who knows and loves him.

Long before they miss me, I think,
the room will be perfectly solid.
When they break in the door and, unsurprised,
hardened to the most bizarre vagaries,
begin to carry out my treasure,
death's what they'll look for underneath it all,
those fluent, muscled, imaginative men,
sweating in their innocent coveralls.

But I will be out in broad daylight by then,
answering,
having accepted utterly the heart's conditions.
Tell them I wish them well, always,
that I've been happy.

COLORADO

Going up or coming down,
I'll give you an earful, the mountain said.
Going up, we stopped at nine thousand feet
under the pressure of that message.

Lake, cabin and stream
are enclosed by the tops of mountains.
The scenery is self-referring,
and here it is best to be provincial,
as in love or avarice.

Whose silly system
tries, every day or two, to scramble higher
toward a bearcave or abandoned mine
in order to look into the mountain?
Mine, pumping and slipping
where pungent rabbitbrush
thrusts up its pubic bush all over
the slope, and Cottonwood Creek
spurts from up there,
its trout hidden as sperm.
Back down in the cabin my bossy heart
tells me for hours how hard it is
to speed up the whole business.

"Rhythmic alternation . . . rocks and lulls attention like the
beating of a silver hammer on metal"

They have taken the silver, those early lovers,
and gone; the half-hour sex hotels
in Leadville, St. Elmo and Buena Vista
are closed. Now, to take in this country,
I must close my eyes, loosen my hold on the pen,
take off my clothes and fall.
One simple agony
and there I'd be, the stream
between my spraddled legs,

foxtail grasses stroking each nerve-end
the whole wild length of my body, hair
tangled in penstemon, buckwheat flower
and tansy aster, chest
pierced by a stand of quaking aspen
straight through the heart, *tremuloides* too.
I'd never get up.

". . . a ghost town of Colorado Mining heyday, it is stirring to
life as a tourist center high in the Rockies"

But look, still humpbacked with slag, the crone
can feel seemly once more, forget and forgive.
Under an ancient, many-turreted hat,
her fresh fluorescent face—
lifted by Sportswear, Sportinggoods
and J. C. Penney—burns,
and her heart is gushing silver again.
Anyone can see. A shameless sign
says "This Way To The Trout Hatchery."

Oh, no one's so innocent this time.
It's possible still, with camper and rod,
to snag out silver and go—
but only so much silver, for a foreknown fee.
What's possible again is some
sophisticated mutual exploitation.

"Affection . . . strikes one with a silence like that of Adam before
he had even named the beasts"

At the end of each slow, ascending S,
we seize from Cottonwood Pass,
each time a bit diminished, the same sight,
an exercise in both return
and aspiration.

Colorado

Twelve thousand feet high, at the top,
there's a small gravelled pull-off, and
(oh yes, we can bring
our bodies along this far)
a tiny toilet of peeled pine.
We stand still, mortal and improbable.
The world is all below us, we can choose
whether to go back down on one side
of the mountain, or the other.

Holding above us a strange snow
that stays for lifetime after lifetime,
the tips of mountains seem like merest hills.
One can almost forget
the wind, the ropes, the cold, the crampons,
avalanches, weaknesses of heart,
but still we only look,
hoping at best to learn a little from the view.
I'll go back down to be
the tourist that I am, and I suppose
that you will too.

"Regular return has . . . the sleep-inducing effect of monotony
. . . poetic ordering has reduced affective pressure"

If I hauled to the top of the hill
my private enterprise,
and, bent to suds of cloud,
washed once and for all
from my lips and eyes
the sexual grimace,
I wouldn't be afraid
to open a silver claim
and try digging with skill
where recurrence has no place,

"The tendency to sleep qualifies, softens . . . so that we are assaulted from a tolerable distance or through a protective screen"

but before that climb,
since I'm so heavily here,
turn away from my face,
my dear and more dear,
and the whore's face of Time.
Rest, and believe
this metrical disgrace:
your heart has kept its silver
and all silver strikes recur.
Sleep, love.
For you I made this rhyme.

WHAT I WANT TO SAY

I

It is as simple as it can be.
I will leave off my clothes
(which is a kind of leveling, isn't it?)
and address you as nakedly
as anyone can.

Each one is perfect,
that is what I want to say.

There is no one perfection,
only an exercise of loving.
And it is always extraordinary.
One wild iris clump,
carried from Maine in a coffee can,
this third year gave me, in the mild summer,
twenty-one exquisite blue flowers.
A showy ten, then a more delicate seven,
then, further down on the stems,
an unlooked-for four.

"Tukaram . . ."
(I am telling you as nakedly as I can)
It happens in time.

When, somewhere, one wave of the sea begins moving,
one moved by the sun, let us say,
the next by the stars, let us say,
the next by the moon,
(I told you you would never believe it)
it is not spent.
It folds back and reenters the sea,
where it is indistinguishable from any other,
the sea who says each time,
"It is what I am."

I I
What do you think love is, anyway?
I'll tell you, a harrowing.
And I stand here helpless with what I know,
because in that Ministry
to be understood leads straight to the room
where understanding stops
and a final scream is that of the self
preserving itself.

To say I love you is a humiliation.
The weak tears gathering in the eyes
drip on a chessboard one fiddles with alone then,
mourning the betrayal of
some other possibility.
It is the absolute narrowing of possibilities,
and everyone, down to the last man,
dreads it.

I I I
It is the eye that calls, as if it were sleepless,
that says in its call, "Come to the window, see,
up there on some moonstruck table-land
a record is turning."

The eye calls the flesh from a sarabande
it is busy composing, "Come, there is something . . .
and not because it is there, because it is not yet there,
and who knows if it is complex, or simple.

That music neither of us can hear,
not transformations but changes,
will move us yet."

THE GOOD MAN

I

It is almost unbearably harmonious—
the purple petunias and stalks of lavender
with a blue couch pillow behind them.
The pillow fastens itself to the flowers
as if there were no space between but blue.
Let beauty fill in spaces where there is no good man.
But if there is a good man, let him put his head
on the blue pillow, and his yellowish face
will interfere with the flowers, and the natural
will become, in an instant, historical, and the historical
will become, in a little while, dramatic.

I I

"A kind of unskillful desire to give life more thickness." GIDE

The dog chews up rye bread and spits it out.
He will do it ten times. It is his humanity.

On the stained and whiskery skin of the world
we walk, bumping shins and knees on things,
but live in our heads, in the sugar and gall
of language, bumping our heads on each other.
If a bird flies down from a tree and lights
on his finger, the good man is surprised.
That is not his forte. He moves words,
and his knees and elbows move to the meaning
of words, through the high stubble of things.

I I I

"How do you *know* a fish doesn't suffer
as much as you do?" the biochemist asked
with anguish. But he was not the good man.
And I too am sickened sometimes by the heaviness
of things to be done. Little roadbuilders, like ants,

swarming to carry away a mountain.
Taking care of a house—to reach the top,
to lift and wash its parts and partitions.
On rainy days my hair gains weight
as if somebody's tears hung in the follicles,
somebody treated unjustly, unthinkingly,
somebody called by the wrong name.
For the good man, to move a mountain one grain
of dust at a time is to move a mountain.
For him the act is laid in the idea
like honey in a honeycomb. We are here for that.
He eats honey without compunction.

THE CHALLENGER

"Perhaps a great love is never returned. Had it been given warmth and shelter by its counterpart in the Other, perhaps it would have been hindered from ever growing to maturity." DAG HAMMARSKJOLD

Old liar, death, do you think I don't see you?
There is not one of your masks I don't know,
even this one, soft and winning—the half-truth.

When the fruit in its bowl turns green I see you, death.
When a sleep-walker hears the clock hands unwind,
when a hand jerks back from a reaching hand.

Even in the motion of rest I touch your face.
I know its shape in love, and in the wit of madness.
I will face up to you, my sleepy lover.

I will fight you with nuance and with clearness,
with the making and breaking of form and measure,
with a greedy face and with an immaculate.

I will lie with clocks, which are always a little late,
I will lie with madness, with the fact that you love me,
and for a long time you will believe me.

RELATIONSHIPS

The legal children of a literary man
remember his ugly words to their mother.
He made them keep quiet and kissed them later.
He made them stop fighting and finish their supper.
His stink in the bathroom sickened their noses.
He left them with sitters in lonesome houses.
He mounted their mother and made them wear braces.
He fattened on fame and raised them thin.

But the secret sons of the same man
spring up like weeds from the seed of his word.
They eat from his hand and it is not hard.
They unravel his sweater and swing from his beard.
They smell in their sleep his ferns and roses.
They hunt the fox on his giant horses.
They slap their mother, repeating his phrases,
and swell in his sight and suck him thin.

TO POETS' WORKSHEETS IN THE
AIR-CONDITIONED VAULT OF A LIBRARY

I

Shall we assume that the world
is waiting to hear how this speech happened,
pretending to be busy about other things,
a housewife on the verge of an affair,
tending the bomb,
clipping in the ruffled borders,
her face rapt and serious, almost saintly,
her poor tempted eyes always looking the other way?
Who can say what the world wants, or waits for?
The only thing we know is so simple
we hardly dare say it.
People keep trying to speak to each other.

II

We are all fools, anyway, of one kind or another,
down on one knee to the imagination,
too scared to do much, in that ridiculous posture,
but hope she didn't hear a creak of the old bones.
Or else convinced she is leaning over our deathbed
while we, like Ralph, whisper our touching and absurd
goodbye: "If you've been hated you've also been loved.
Ah but, dear Lady, *adored!*"
When all the long love-lorn while
the problem was one of believing our own recognitions,
no doubt the greatest foolishness of all.
May one note here, nevertheless, that to believe them
is occasionally useful?

III

Without turning the light on,
somebody snatched five words from a nightmare
in the scrawl of a blind Titan.
Up the Christmas list,

past the black currant jelly and over the electric sander,
a little judgment meanders.
Trying to say it, trying to say,
the typewriter sputters its clogged e
into a big printed HAPPY BIRTHDAY DADDY.
A minnow flipped out of the eye's pond
into this bar napkin
which keeps it moistened.
Twenty Xed-out lines and "Oh hell with it. Oh shit."
The slapped mouth reddens
on a yellow second-sheet.

I V

I woke last night
to see these leaves falling through the air,
and in its labor,
letting its leaves fall, yellow and white,
the mind standing like a tree,
suffering its changes.
And I seemed to hear in a half-sleep
something feeding and pressing up
from the ground where this waste fell,
something fruited and gentle.

V

That body gracing the sofa with such a studied sprawl,
smoking a cigarette to kill the taste of the last
heart-of-artichoke marinated in a court bouillon,
two fingers twitching at its imported, unfamiliar,
badly tied ascot
and talking about Malcolm Muggeridge—
who could guess that this very moment in its heart-of-hearts
it wants to be halfway across the country
kissing the eyelids of someone it's never been introduced to,
saying, "You interest me strangely."
Saying, "Nobody has ever listened to me like this before."

VI

Stay, then, in that cool place.
The world itself creates
possibility after possibility,
constantly erupts, and quiets.

When shape and shapeliness come together
in a quiet ceremony of chance,
page after page will finally be delivered
into the perfect hands.

THE TWINS

My sweet-faced, tattle-tale brother was born blind,
but the colors drip in his head. He paints with his fingers.
All day with his pots and paper he follows me around
wherever I set up my easel, till I pinch his bat ears,

then before he goes he swears he didn't feel anything.
But he knows my feelings, sneaks them out of my skin.
The things he knows! Leaving me squeezed and sulking,
he pretends he felt them himself and tells everyone.

Nobody ever blames him. He's terribly talented.
The world, glimpsing itself through him, will grow
sick with self-love, it seems, and under his eyelid
lie down, in burning shame, with its own shadow,

whereas, on my canvas, it wears its gray and brown
like a fat beaver, and even as I sweat on my brush,
all forms, at its simple-minded toothy grin,
branches, limbs, trunks, topple in a watery backwash.

When he goes to sleep, he says, the world stays in his head
like a big spiderweb strung between ear and ear,
buzzing like telephone wires, and what he has heard
all night, next morning has happened, is true, is there.

Though it always comes back for me, thick, bathed, grateful,
everything has to be re-imagined each sunrise
when I crawl from my black comfort. But I can't make a phone
    call.
I have to talk to something in front of my eyes.

You'd never know we were close. When we meet strangers
they poke my round stomach and pat his long bare legs,
I gush, and he, or that's what it looks like, glares,
then he stomps on my oils and we fight like cats and dogs.

But when it rains sometimes, and he feels it and I hear it,
and he closes my eyes with his fingers to stop my raining,
and one tear falls before everything is quiet,
and his tear is the color of cinnamon on my tongue,

oh then we leave together and nobody can find us.
Not even our mother, if she came, could tell us apart.
Only the stars can see, who cluster around us,
my painted person crouched in his painted heart.

LEDA RECONSIDERED

She had a little time to think
as he stepped out of water
that paled from the loss of his whiteness
and came toward her.
A certain wit in the way he
handled his webbed feet,
the modesty of the light that lay on him,
a perfectly clear, and unforgiveable,
irony in the cock of his head
told her more than he knew.
She sat there in the sunshine,
naked as a new-hatched bird,
watching him come,
trying to put herself
in the place of the cob, and see
what he saw:

flesh comfortable, used,
but still neatly following the bones,
a posture relaxed,
almost unseemly, expressing
(for the imagination,
unlike the poor body it strips and stirs,
is never assaulted)
openness, complicity even,
the look of a woman
with a context in which she can put
what comes next
(no chance of maiden's hysteria
if his beak pinched hold of her neck-skin,
yet the strangeness of the thing
could still startle her
into new gestures,)
and something—a heaviness,
as if she could bear things,

or as if, when he fertilized her,
he were seeding the bank she sat on,
the earth in its aspect of
quiescence.

And now, how much would she try
to see, to take,
of what was not hers, of what
was not going to be offered?
There was that old story
of matching him change for change,
pursuing, and at the solstice
devouring him.
A man's story.
No, she was not that hungry
for experience. She had her loves.
To re-imagine her life—
as if the effort were muscular
she lifted herself a little
and felt the pull at neck
and shoulderblade, back
to the usual.
And suppose she reached with practiced arms
past the bird, short of the god,
for a vulnerable mid-point,
and held on,
just how short-sighted would that
be? Would the heavens in a flurry record
a major injustice to the world's
possibilities?

He took his time,
pausing to shake out a wing.
The arrogance of that gesture!
And yet she saw him
as the true god.

She saw, with mortal eyes
that stung at the sight,
the pain of his transformations,
which, beautiful or comic,
came to the world
with the risk of the whole self.
She saw what he had to work through
as he took, over and over,
the risk of love,
the risk of being held,
and saw to the bare heart
of his soaring, his journeying,
his wish for the world
whose arms he could enter in the image
of what is brave or golden.

To love with the whole imagination—
she had never tried.
Was there a form for that?
Deep, in her inmost, grubby
female center
(how could he know that,
in his airiness?)
lay the joy of being used,
and its heavy peace, perhaps,
would keep her down.
To give: women and gods
are alike in enjoying that ceremony,
find its smoke filling and sweet.
But to give up was an offering
only she could savor,
simply by covering
her eyes.

He was close to some uncommitted
part of her.
Her thoughts dissolved and
fell out of her body like dew
onto the grass of the bank,
the small wild flowers,
as his shadow,
the first chill of his ghostliness,
fell on her skin.
She waited for him so quietly that
he came on her quietly,
almost with tenderness,
not treading her.
Her hand moved into the dense plumes
on his breast to touch
the utter stranger.

THE VOYEUR

The sizzle of the Coleman
seals off fir, birch and underbrush
with their mixed bag of onlookers who
scuffle at the edge, held back
by light from claiming garbage
and clearing as wild favors,
and detaches both the path to the lake,
crossed sometimes by deer or partridge
in lunatic self-absorption,
and its continuance,
a chill path the moon
laid down over the heads of simple-minded
swimmers, from the cabin's
hot work of being human.
Pants and bra dangle
from one hand. On the kitchen wall
behind her the machines of her usefulness,
washed and hung up, take on a glittery, ornamental life,
the book, in a gnat-specked circle
of white brilliance, is closed,
the vacant half of a bed
beside her, open. She faces
the window, wondering
what encroachments, if any,
will take place this night.

Like the pinch of a deerfly
she feels flank, then throat
lit on, focussed on,
and, shading her eyes at the glass,
makes out, mid-path, something big that the moon
is back of, neither the stilted poise
of a deer, nor a bear's upright,
goofy and amiable-looking
assessment of darkness,

but something the night wizens,
something hunched.
And so she believes its gaze
belongs to her, that its feeding
is abstract enough to overlook
the clearing's juicy tufts,
bitten flesh and bones in the garbage,
and fall on hers. Matchmaker
for the ark of this moment,
she selects a shape
out of the great plenty of the woods
to get along with.

She straightens, but stays,
and lowers her eyes, lest their looks,
hers and the other's,
lock and fall down together, wrestling
in the shrubby borderline between them,
suddenly feeling herself
so showy, so lighted,
she wants his eyes to find the
pure recipience she has turned to
and bring it . . . what? Anything,
sweet, sacred, or evil,
in his attention.
Slowly, arms over head,
she begins to enter a new dress,
her nakedness, steam-fitted
by his eye to each slope and point.
She is entering it
with the whole imagination contracted
to him, to what he sees,
and as her breasts swell and press
on cups of a fabric unfashionably
sleek, as belly, thighs,
wrists, ankles are being contained
in his donation,

she believes if he winked
out there in the moonlight
one side of her would go numb.

The gassy, effusive lamp
holds its breath until
she has been wholly seen,
until this first act of creation's
perfect little comedy is over.
When it throws against the wall
her humpy twin of dark dough,
handled for twenty years,
she has shed their kinship,
she has shed belief
that the strongest love is habitual.
As at dusk on the beach
a sandal slipping squeezes out
from between rocks a green air,
so she feels herself flavored.
A tongue, touched between neck and shoulder
would find the wild mint.

Feeling too clear,
she hides behind her arms
and leans to the window.
He slinks into the black clutter
beside the path.
Given her form and left to find
its function, she'd like to see him now,
rock at the bait of her breast
his cheek, whose stubble
would snag the fresh silk,
wipe his wet mouth with her lips,

The Voyeur

           return under his grip
           to creased, to rumpled
           thing that manhood mounts,
           go into the woods even
           to claim an animal who couldn't
           believe his eyes.

ALONG THE ROAD

The ticker tapes roll down my sides
with the same quotation: midsummer;
field green, pine green; market steady.
For three days I have taken on faith
continuous, complicated negotiations
of the pricked-eared, calculating-eyed
under, let us say, ferns, cattails,
and profitable buzz in, surely, fieldflowers,
clover, as I take on faith
on the longest expressway
the courting embraces of father and mother,
congressional pity, presidential wisdom,
the entrance of bullets into real flesh,
over and over, the end of my life.
But now one ribbon breaks for a flaming
moment, cheek, shoulder, rib, hip
turn hot. Wait. Onto the green,
glazed retina comes
an explosion of hurled orange.
They are burning the dump.
Even in the afterthoughts, black, gray,
seeping through the sky like rivers
feeling out new beds, damping down
tops of trees and a steeple, threatening
to inundate a hillful of little houses
in pebble colors, the eye turns
back where something was seen.
Stay there with me, my dear,
free from the reticence
of ordinary incineration, and watch.
During the first days there will be
only an interruption, gorgeous, mutual,
of the texture and temperature of the world,
a representation by three of its acres
of uproar, extravagance, primitivism, seething,

and our senses will tire from it
as they tire from any other
overmastering abundance, yet
we will use memory and imagination
to inform ourselves that it is a process
of reduction. In its center
something serious is happening.
This is what I want you to wait for.
When the flames lower themselves onto
their fearful bed, draw in on themselves,
devote themselves with unbelievable intensity
to this consummation, it is important
that your eyes and my eyes be wide open,
unchilled, immodest, focussed outward.
On the edge—we notice it together—the first
disclosure. Its spasms of hot white breath
stop. It is innocent of color,
and so without insinuation,
without suppliance. Black. Formal. Wry.
Black spirals spray up
over a black hummock and bent black bars
jam the entrances to black caverns,
while the mind runs backward for a last
reconstruction: springs and bones
have been bitten from their fat,
barrels, cans, cars
set free from the need to contain.
All over the area there goes on
a slow, entranced emergence
of things out of the ashes of their usefulness.
There is nothing seasonal here.
If we have lost sight of comfort,
of fleshy, vegetable consolations,
still we have arrived at an entanglement
of true weight, a landscape of certainties.

(Will you smile with me at one corner
where the lamp cranes its neck like an outraged hen
hearing indecencies from an egg
of a kettle beside it? The comic keeps.)
Let us make sure now
that no amount of imagining
could have furnished us with the particular
fusion over there, this antic
tin stretch, that petrified
moment of rage when something tried
to ooze out of its own nature,
eyeful by eyeful the exact, extensive
derangement. When you turn away, remember
none of this needs to be taken on faith;
it was all there when we were both looking.
Now let us go, each to his own
assumptions. Out of long habit
I myself will continue to suppose
that the planet can see out of either eye,
can subsidize its creatures with dark
as well as with light (though only
by squeak, snap and hoot have I ever envisioned
the night life of the woods)
and when it rolls
(I suppose, don't you, that it rolls?)
it may even be able to feel, bearing down
on its side, the contribution we've just
witnessed, our heavy,
drossless, dark deposit.
And though I turn and take stock again
in its indefinite green, out of long habit
I will continue to say
we were dealing back there at the dump with the planet's
shapeliest, least abstract business.

IV

"*From perfect Grief there need not be Wisdom or even memory.*"

MARRIAGE, WITH BEASTS

for Jarvis

Bringing our love to the zoo to see what species
it is, I carry my head under my arm,
you cradle yours; we will hold them up to cages
or set them back on perch at the proper moments.
Each inch of my skin tingles, and I guess
yours tingles, as in high fever or sex heat
it is also reminded of its old bestial uses,
for what happens here is as informal
as disease, and we, like lust, are serious
about making sense of a strange, entire surface.

We consider first a herd of some big bruisers
who toddle around in tap-shoes, musing, grazing,
slim of hip and giant at head and shoulders
like football players ready to butt or shove.
As unselfconsciously as trees drip mosses
they dangle tatters of their worn-out winter coats
and neither marry nor burn, being as couplers
wholly impersonal. "Intraspecific aggression"
is simply not in them. Clearer than we suppose
our lowered heads can speak, they speak: Lorenz.
A murderous rage is the force that through green fuses
drives the daisies of love. Why yes, sweet mate,
your face and dress are dearer than anyone else's.
Why yes, life's light, we could kill each other with pillows.

Then come, my Moor in embryo, and let us
look at the birds and tease our remarkable hearts
with flocks of bright little resemblances.
Behind the glass they fly as if they were free,
and flash like multi-colored fingernails
of fingers that reach to all the keys of the air
and sound them for us. Holding such weight in our headbowls,
such stuffing, not of straw, but metaphors,
how can we scoop up these endless symphonies?

Lifted to birds, my scoop at least reminds you
to see through the great discrepancy of size
and find our own disorder, a birds-eye view.
My dear, your head heavily says, though earth
receives as "a tiny burden" a bird's death,
the burden swells, for one other bird, to despair
the size of the world. My dearest, mine replies,
the size of the world, sun, moon and stars
for the little while that he waits alone in bare
ruins of the choir where last she sang
and trills, but much too late, Oh stay, thou art fair.

At the pond we put on our heads, for the fowl here
will make us feel at home for a moment, being
the big-boned and aetherial mixed together.
Under such wings Leda conceived, and in
her lap "erst empfand er glücklich sein Gefieder."
The flamingo, testing each of his distant footsteps,
looks like the Duc de Guermantes, who trembles and teeters
on the high stilts of his eighty or more years.
Think how we've raised our own eyes from the ground
and tell me if we must tuck our heads in a wing,
my chilling redbreast, or watch the swans mount air
and take from their gyres terror or comforting.

At a farther pond we're going past, a "wallow
of flesh" lifts up its simple putty face. "Blou-
augh!" it says to me. Does it say that to you?

Shall we stop and find out if the monkeys wink too much?
As at Charenton, we hear these fools gibber,
and my head, that watches the "watched spectator" see
them throwing dung and garbage at one another,
grins, then ducks back in the lair of my arms
as your eyes pelt it with revulsion and pity.

Headstrong now, we enter the Nursery door
with a crowd of parents and children. My famished lover,
see how the tiger kit lays back his ears
for the bliss of his bottle. See, inside the oven
of the incubator, each wolf like a new-baked bun.
What can I feed you but old love over again?
That monkey mite, you say, I was thinking, rather,
how he hung like a rare sweet medal on his mother
as she swung up to the bars in a line by Swenson.
Tell me, my own perverse heroine,
making a public display of how bare you are,
what necklace of love can I ever bring you to wear?
The cubs box, but we stop their show. On either
side of the glass the charming babies stare
and whimper to see two grown-ups rocking each other.

In the raw, menstrual smell of the lion house
we go for a last stroll. Nemerov sparrows
make free with kings, being willing to eat their shit.
As far distant as they can get from the hose
that flushes away bones, flies and urine,
snooting the praise of their dumpy audience,
the cats stride with the strained hauteur of fashion
models, back and forth, rippling their coats.
We're tired of disguises, but what else can we look at?
Wait. A mountain lion stops and gazes
at me. He comes straight at me up to the bars
and stays there, looking me in the eye. He neither
implores nor threatens, he is only after some sight.
I see the slit in his iris. I think of Jeffers'
obsessed will to arrive at the inhuman
view, of Dickey, who began to act out his own
animal when he caught the eye of a panther.
A lightening whirl, snarl, rake at her face
with his spiked paw, and the lion discounts his mate,
coming up to see. She leaves. He sees me alone.

But I've lost my head, it rolls on the floor in spit
and candy wrappers, spilling. I get it back on.
Something, through his eye-slit, irradiates
my bones to simmering heat. In stillness. What is it?
No god is there. I feel nothing Ledean.
What can it be that comes without images?
An eye, nothing in it but what he is,
the word, then,
     after all this,
         not love but

LION?
The slit widens. There. Illiterate.
Perfect. lion. without adjective.
lion lionlionlion it ceases
to be a word

  but I get away, turning to where you are.
I'm shaking. Now take what you've seen of me home, and let's
go on with our heady life. And treat me, my pet,
forever after as what I seem; for it seems,
and it is, impossible for me to receive,
under the cagey wedlock of your eyes,
what I make it impossible for you to give.

MONA VAN DUYN

Mona Van Duyn (Mrs. Jarvis Thurston) was born in Waterloo, Iowa in 1921 and now lives in St. Louis. She studied and taught in the University of Iowa Writers' Workshop in the 1940's and has taught writing and literature at the University of Louisville and Washington University. With her husband she founded *Perspective, a Quarterly of Literature* in 1947, and is still its co-editor. She has received the Eunice Tietjens award (1956) and the Harriet Monroe Award (1968) from *Poetry*, the Helen Bullis Prize (1964) from *Poetry Northwest*, the Hart Crane Memorial Award from The American Weave Press (1968), and first prize in the Borestone Mountain Awards Volume (1968); she was one of the first five American poets to be given a grant from the National Foundation for the Arts. In 1971 she was awarded the National Book Award in Poetry for the present volume.

DATE DUE

GAYLORD			PRINTED IN U.S.A.